WELCOME

Person & Planet by Purevant Living is a
publication that shares all things good within
sustainability and wellness including articles,
company highlights, new product development,
organizations, public policy, wellness and eco
tips, recipes, artwork, and photography.

This publication is a valuable resource for
businesses and consumers alike, to educate
readers on sustainable solutions for the
planet and personal health.

SUBSCRIBE
News & Updates
Subscribe at purevantliving.com

PODCAST
To Listen:
anchor.fm/personandplanet

SUBMISSIONS
To submit a written or art contribution, please
send to submissions@purevantliving.com

SPONSORS
To inquire about sponsorship and advertisements,
please contact sk@purevantliving.com

For questions, contact personandplanet@purevantliving.com

CONTRIBUTORS

Alexis Arnold
Photographer

Steve Brandt
Photographer

Francesca Busca
Artist

Tricia Carey
Interviewee

Nicole Conrad
Photographer

Jake Disraeli
Interviewee

Matthias Heilig
Writer, Photographer

Brooke Hodgson
Writer

Amanda Hofacker
Writer

Devrim Furkan Kavcar
Artist

Joe Krubsack
Photographer

Stephanie Krubsack
Writer, Photographer

Cindi Lockhart, RDN, LD
Writer

Deagan Maki
Writer

Dr. Tiffany Mullen
Writer

Jennifer Nowicki
Writer

Louise Ellwood Parker
Artist

Shaena Ragna
Photographer

Megan Rorabeck
Writer

Molly Sommerhalder
Writer

Paulien Wesselink
Interviewee

Ike Wynter
Interviewee, Artist

LETTER FROM THE EDITOR

Dear Reader,

Words cannot express how thankful I am that you're choosing to read the first issue of Person & Planet by Purevant Living! I tear up just thinking about all of the amazing work being done, honored to share those stories in this publication and on the Person & Planet Podcast. It is hard to express in words the joy I feel when working with all who contributed to this issue, including the amazing initiatives each individual or organization creates and stands for, sharing actionable wellness and eco tips, products and services, and creating a resource to help each of us live healthier, more sustainable lives.

Although we encourage you to select the digital option, we know that there is no replacement for a physical copy, something to hold, share, and refer to again and again. We have chosen print on demand via Amazon, with the goal to move to a C2C certified printer in the near future as the publication grows. After running the figures, printing only the exact quantity and shipping from the printer directly to the reader is the most carbon friendly option, versus double shipping with other services. You can feel good about your purchase however, because we have a commitment to donate 2% of every sale. We joined the Wisconsin Sustainable Business Council, 1% For The Planet, and Carbonfree® Partner Program for small businesses to show commitment to environmental conservation, to build a structure for giving back. Through these actions we are able to offset our annual carbon footprint from all operations.

Each quarterly publication will include a sustainability, art, wellness, and recipe section, with included photography throughout. In an ode to "Highlights" magazine and fond childhood memories, I wanted to bring a bit of joy to each issue, including a coloring or activity page for adults and children alike. In addition, each issue will also include a small dictionary of terms mentioned throughout the articles, for reference and a better explanation. Please enjoy the contents, to learn and be inspired to create positive change!

Thank you for caring about person and planet,

Stephanie Krubsack

CONTENTS

ISSUE 1

PERSON & PLANET

SPRING 2022

CONTENTS

CONTENTS

RECIPES

ACTIVITIES

ISSUE 1

PERSON & PLANET

SPRING 2022

Art is a Journey, Let's Make It Sustainable, "Hope is taking action" -Greta Thunberg, by Devrim Furkan Kavcar, sustainable art arrangement with dry flowers and leaves.

INNOVATIVE BY NATURE

TENCEL™: A TENACIOUS FIBER REDEFINING THE TEXTILE & FASHION INDUSTRY

Plants from nature supply us with a multitude of things including food, shelter, clothing and so much more. Trees are one of the most important renewable resources, traditionally used as wood for building, but when broken down into fibers called cellulose, the possibilities unfold.

Lenzing Group, headquartered in Austria, began sourcing materials from nature over 80 years ago, creating renewable fibers for textiles to be developed into fashion and beauty products. According to Tricia Carey, Director of Global Business Development Denim and Americas at Lenzing Group, the fiber called TENCEL™ has an important meaning in itself. She stated, "Our fibers have strong tenacity, and that's where the word TENCEL™ comes from, the TEN is for tenacity and the CEL is cellulose." Cellulose is a product derived from the wood pulp of trees, including the bark, branches, and leaves of the plant.

At Lenzing Group there are actually three TENCEL™ fibers including Lyocell, Modal, and Lyocell Filament. Each is made from a form of wood fiber.

FIBERS & FORESTRY

The pulp fibers for these textiles are extracted first from sustainably grown trees including beech, eucalyptus, birch, and spruce. Lenzing Group even developed a process where transitioning the pulp into cellulose fibers is done energy efficiently via their biorefinery. In this process, remaining byproducts of the trees are used as bioenergy to create the end product forming a closed loop manufacturing process. Even further, at least 99.5% of the solvents used during product development are reused in addition to other resource-conserving technologies during production.

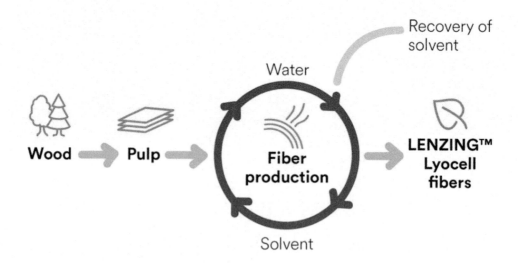

Tricia Carey stated, "It's how we can still feel that we are making sure that we're leaving the lowest footprint possible, but it all goes back to the consumption levels to start with. I would like people to know that it's the small steps that we can take, that it's the progress that we make, not always thinking of the perfection of where it ultimately needs to be."

This renewable textile is also biodegradable or compostable, making it a true circular product. With a closed loop manufacturing process, the product's creation and end of life is taken into account, coming from the earth and going back into the earth as organic matter.

Since the fibers come from trees, TENCEL™ is considered a natural fiber from a renewable resource. More importantly, for the decomposition process of the material, it can even be composted at home. Some materials require commercial composting centers to be fully biodegradable, which can include industrial sized equipment with heat processing and of course the availability of those facilities.

DENIM & CIRCULAR FASHION

The "innovative by nature" slogan truly highlights the Lenzing fibers including the TENCEL™ Modal which is known for its soft texture and flexibility, where TENCEL™ Lyocell is known to be moisture-wicking and breathable in fabrics. Some denim brands that integrate TENCEL™ fibers into their  designs include Boyish Jeans and Kings of Indigo. The fibers are so versatile that brands such as Levi, H&M, Uniqlo, Lululemon, Nike, and Allbirds even use them too.

"Denim brands are looking at biodegradability, what is happening at that end of use, if it's not going to be resold, what happens to it. That's where we look at even our products, they are compostable or biodegradable and go back to nature," according to Carey. Due to the fact that 20% of the over 100 billion garments produced every year go unused, she encourages the mindset to, "buy less buy better." Carey further elaborates that it's important to, "Know what you're buying, know who you're buying from, and also be responsible when you're discarding it. When you no longer want it, how can you keep that garment in circulation? Is there someone you can give it to? Is there a charity? How can you recycle textiles? Don't just throw it in the garbage. Only 15% of textiles are being recycled."

Circularity is further defined by resale, the popularity of vintage clothing, and even companies that combine old and new to create something redesigned, found in brands like RE/DONE® and others who repurpose or recycle materials.

You can learn more about circulatory in the textile industry at Lenzing Group, and more on the denim industry from the Carved in Blue blog, Blue Cast podcast, and Blue Lenz video channel where Tricia Carey interviews guests in all areas of textile development and product creation, specifically for denim brands and innovators.

Fridays For Future Global Climate Strike to demand for intersectional climate justice, Konstanz, Germany, September 2021.

Fridays For Future Global Climate Strike to demand for
intersectional climate justice, Konstanz, Germany,
September 2021.

Fridays For Future Global Climate Strike to demand for
intersectional climate justice, Konstanz, Germany,
September 2021.

THE POSITIVE FOOTPRINT: HOW CRADLE TO CRADLE CAN CHANGE THE WAY WE PRODUCE, BUILD AND UNDERSTAND OUR ROLE AS HUMANS ON THE PLANET

by Matthias Heilig; photography by Nicole Conrad

We all know about the tremendous ecological crisis we are facing right now in the world: The rapid progression of man-made global warming, the excessive pollution of natural habitats and oceans, deforestation, threatening mass extinction and the loss of soil and resources. Therefore, we are currently losing the ability to fulfill the needs of future generations. Sustainable development can be defined as a way to meet the needs of today without compromising the ability to fulfill the needs of tomorrow. Accordingly, the majority of our economy and the way we produce things now "from cradle to grave" is very contrary to the concept of sustainability. Every year, we overuse our natural resources after the so-called "Earth Overshoot Day", which was surpassed in 2020 on the 22nd of

August, even during the global pandemic while a big part of the global economy was shut down. What can we do to escape this depressing dilemma? What is our role as intelligent beings on this planet? Are we determined to negatively impact the environment forever or is there a way to re-think and re-engineer everything once again to create a truly sustainable future?

THE CRADLE TO CRADLE-VISION

We live in a world where the concept of "waste" as such does not exist anymore. Using nature as an example, all materials are kept endlessly within closed circles, powered by renewable energies only. All used materials serve as nutrients for new biological or technical products. We have overcome the destructive ways of manufacturing and building and our limited belief of being only consumers of the earth. Being just "less bad" was not satisfying anymore and we have realized our potential to be truly beneficial for the planet and society in manifold ways. Therefore, we create a positive impact in the way we design, produce and build, wherever possible. Our buildings use and deliver renewable energy, increase biodiversity, capture carbon, purify water, purify air and are healthy habitats for humans and animals - just like trees. A city consisting of such buildings is a living and prosperous oasis for humans and nature - just like a forest. Farming, whether it is in rural or in urban areas, produces healthy soil and supports a huge variety of animals and insects. All materials used are well known (positively defined or whitelisted) and chosen carefully to be healthy. We celebrate diversity in society and technology while practicing a healthy and supportive way of living together. This is the world we want to live in!

THE CRADLE TO CRADLE-DESIGN PRINCIPLES

Whenever a product turns into trash at the end of its lifespan, the product is based on a faulty design concept. Therefore, product designers need to think ahead for the product lifespan to prevent materials from ever turning into "useless trash". All materials have to be kept within the technological circle (e.g. metals, plastics, chemicals, glass) or the biological cycle (e.g. cotton, wood, biodegradables, paper, leather) and

the two circles should never be mixed up inseparably. Cradle to Cradle (C2C) distinguishes between products that are being used, like bicycles, TVs, washing machines and cars, which belong to the technical cycle, and products that are consumed and/or are subjected to abrasion, like clothing, shoe soles, brake pads, seat covers, cosmetics, one-way packaging, which needs to belong to the biological circle. A t-shirt produced with organic cotton and colored with biodegradable colors (free of heavy metals) can be recycled or composted easily at the end of its lifespan. Natural fibers can be reused many times before they can be turned into nutrition for plants. An aluminum frame used for a bicycle can be recycled in primary quality after the frame is not usable anymore. Even better, the frame could be reused again for a new bicycle and other parts could be replaced. Packaging material

"Sustainable development can be defined as a way to meet the needs of today without compromising the ability to fulfill the needs of tomorrow."

for ice cream could be biodegradable and may even contain seeds of rare local plants. Customers who buy such products would be even beneficial to the environment if the packaging is lost in a forest. Instead of selling washing machines, companies could rent them out and offer the service of washing to their customers. In this way, manufacturers can use the best long-lasting materials available instead of producing low quality products that may just survive their warranty time (planned obsolescence). In order to maintain a circular economy, we need to use 100% renewable energy from solar, wind and thermal energy sources. Hydrocarbons (plastics) should be used only for necessary applications (e.g. in medicine) and could be recycled within the technological cycle, if they are kept pure. Architects should think outside of the box to create buildings like trees with positive emissions and benefits instead of harming the environment. Buildings can act as material banks, where all the used building materials are well documented and are being preserved for future generations.

WHAT CAN I DO TO INCREASE MY POSITIVE FOOTPRINT NOW?

Of course, it is always good to start with reducing unnecessary emissions and consumption whenever possible and as long as we can compromise with the implied constraints. Shrinking the negative footprint is the common approach of many eco-philosophies (sufficiency, consistency and efficiency), which is a very good starting point. C2C wants to go beyond the limited understanding of just reducing the harmful impacts and open up to the possibilities to create effective benefits for society and the environment. There is a growing number of C2C-certified products and building materials available that we can already choose today. These companies, even though they might not be perfect today, have committed themselves to constantly improve on the following five C2C-criteria: Material Health, Material Reutilization, Renewable Energy & Carbon Management, Water Stewardship and Social Fairness. Social Fairness along the whole supply chain of manufacturing is a prerequisite for true sustainability, as it can only maintain the balance between ecology, economy and social equity. As customers we have a bigger impact on production than we might think by choosing more sustainable products and demanding more C2C solutions from companies. As entrepreneurs we can choose to transform our business and be C2C-inspired, with or without a certification. Do your best, offset the rest: We can easily offset our residual carbon emissions caused by our daily lives and travels by supporting climate protection organizations or tree planting projects. At home we can use biodegradable soaps, organic clothing, chairs that can be completely recycled, or eat more plant-based food to shrink our negative footprint. Support biodiversity in your garden and in your city by planting various plants and providing bee hives or insect hotels. Investing your money in sustainable companies that support a transition to a carbon-free industry (renewable energies, electro mobility, plant-based food, sustainable infrastructure) has a bigger impact than you might think. Most people are not conscious about what their money in the bank account is used for and many banks still support the old fashioned fossil industries with their financial products. The possibilities to create a positive footprint are just limited by our imagination. Even more can be done to support a faster transition into a real circular and

sustainable economy: Be active, informed and talk about C2C with your colleagues and friends and most importantly with your local politicians. Demand more C2C solutions from politicians and companies directly - every voice counts much more than one might think. Politics need to set the framework to support good companies that are already part of the transition to sustainability or plan to develop positive footprint solutions. Within the population, awareness of the necessity to act now is growing fast (e.g. the Fridays for Future movement on climate justice) and this is strongly reflected in politician's decisions, who try to stay in power. That's why the C2C NGO (Cradle to Cradle non-government organization) was founded in Germany. We inform and teach about Cradle to Cradle in schools, universities and markets and create more awareness about the C2C philosophy and principles. We influence our politicians to act now for a better and more sustainable future! Become part of our mission and share the solutions of tomorrow.

Sources:
Cradle to Cradle: Remaking the Way We Make Things | Book from 2002, by Michael Braungard & William McDonough
C2Ccertified.org | Cradle to Cradle Products Innovation Institute – Oakland, CA
C2C-centre.com | Venlo City Hall in Netherlands as a good example of C2C-architecture
Epea.com | C2C-consulting and innovation partner in Hamburg, Germany
C2C.ngo | non-profit organization founded in Germany to spread the awareness about C2C
Overshootday.org | Information about the global (over)use of resources

The beautiful Donau (Danube) River Valley in
Beuron, Germany.

Goji the
Robin, by
Louise Ellwood
Parker, acrylic
paint and ink
on driftwood.

O MY BAG: ECO & ETHICAL BAGS IN THE GLOBAL MARKET

With a passion for ethical trade originating from a childhood project on developing countries, Paulien Wesselink began her journey as a social entrepreneur by creating O My Bag, a fairly made and eco-friendly leather bag company in Amsterdam.

Driven to create a positive global impact, she shared that, "A very large part of the world is really unequally structured and one of the reasons is the way we do business, especially in international trade. Since this is something we are creating ourselves, it is also something we can be the solution for."

Wesselink first traveled to the source of leather production in Kolkata, India, an area with over 15,000 one-room factories. Upon visiting several of these leather factories and meeting the workers, this solidified the desire to produce products in a sustainable and ethical manner, providing fair wages so workers could support their families. As part of the solution, the goal to create even more jobs under good labor conditions and more opportunities for women enabled the connection of these small

> "It is possible to conduct business in a different way and also be profitable and grow while not harming the planet and its people."

producers to the global market. Even the O My Bag code of conduct clearly defines requirements for manufacturing partners which protect human rights, prevents discrimination and many more policies in protection of the workers and the environment. Wesselink stated, "It is possible to conduct business in a different way and also be profitable and grow while not harming the planet and its people." She combined her love for fair trade and the environment with designing beautiful bags, to create a brand with passion and purpose.

WEAR A DIFFERENCE

With their slogan, "Wear a difference," consumers are encouraged to make a statement through what they purchase and wear, from brands that want to positively impact the people involved in their processes, to the environment. Holding the responsibility to take action on the sustainability principles can seem daunting, but O My Bag founder Paulien Wesselink wants everyone to realize that individual action makes an impact. She explained that, "Where you spend your money really makes a difference in the world. Every time you buy something you cast a vote for the world you want to live in. Do you buy things that exploit the environment or do you try to spend consciously and support companies that invest in the environment?" Each of us has that power, to challenge how things are done and to encourage companies to make fair and sustainable business decisions.

SUSTAINABILITY TERMS & DESIGN

One such business decision that O My Bag actively practices is reducing and limiting their environmental footprint, or carbon emissions created during manufacturing and operations. These emissions could be formed from transportation of materials and goods and the energy needed for processing the products. Insetting is first

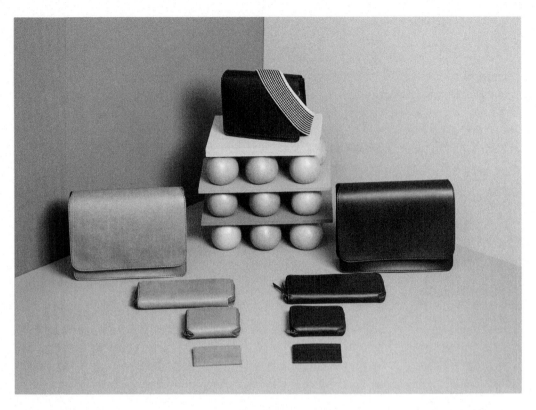

implemented, to reduce emissions within the company's value or supply chain before offsetting through monetary or other means. To help reduce the amount of emissions, recycled cotton is used for 30% of the total cotton needed for the bag liners and the remaining is virgin cotton in order to maintain material strength. Using recycled products when possible is less harmful to the environment during the treatment process using water.

When using water during manufacturing, it is released back into the environment as effluent water or sometimes called wastewater. In this case, O My Bag wanted to be sure that the water released was as clean as possible, not using chromium during the leather tanning process. Effluent water can be hazardous in India, often ending up in drinking water and in the water used for crops, so this risk was avoided.

Trade not aid is a common phrase that O My Bag also stands for, working to promote free trade and development in the global marketplace versus sending direct aid. Through this model, more and higher paying jobs are created in addition to training and higher standards for working conditions. Wesselink shared that, "Having a decent job is crucial for wellbeing, not only because of the pay but because it gives a sense of belonging, accomplishment and purpose...what we're big on at O My Bag."

THE MAKING OF THE PERFECT BAG

The O My Bag brand mission is to leave a positive impact on the world both for people and the planet. What began as a social concept to support trade, later developed into a two-part mission for fair trade and eco ethics.

On their path towards fashion sustainability and first realizing that the leather tanning industry didn't match fair trade values, they convinced producers to create a product under more sustainable and ethical practices. After paving the way over 10 years ago to create a more eco-friendly method of leather tanning, Wesselink said, "It was interesting to see how we had a small part in changing the leather industry as a whole around Kolkata," explaining that quality and fashion could go hand in hand.

Later, when developing a vegan leather option, AppleSkin™ was decided upon to avoid extracting more raw materials or using fake leather made from PU polyurethane plastic. This is a new, more eco-friendly way of alternative leather production, which uses byproducts of the apples, from the applesauce and apple juice industry, just as leather or hide is a byproduct of the meat and dairy industry. The fair trade and ethically made bags continue to be innovative and carbon conscious.

CIRCULARITY

O My Bag also has a secondhand program intended to keep bags in circulation longer, where customers can sell back an older bag and even exchange for credit towards a new bag. Their Pre-loved library is available to everyone online, and there are also in-store pre-loved sections at each brick and mortar location.

Now a Certified B Corporation®, we think we know why they say at O My Bag, "Hold my bag while I change the world."

Photography by Steve Brandt.

FIBER-BASED PACKAGING FOR BETTER END-OF-LIFE

by Deagan Maki

The paper industry has gone through many phases throughout the last 174 years. Paper and fiber-based packaging is now at the cutting-edge of developing solutions that will eventually replace non-renewable packages, contents, containers, and more. From compostability to recyclability, paper products, when produced utilizing sustainably managed forests, can have a positive end-of-life result.

Ahlstrom-Munksjö, a fiber-based solutions paper company, has worked diligently to go "back to the basics" of papermaking by using fewer chemicals, finding natural ingredient alternatives, and educating consumers and brands on the use of fiber-based packaging solutions as opposed to non-renewable substrates. Ahlstrom-Munksjö has a global manufacturing platform, but the roots of their Wisconsin, U.S. plants run deep. Wisconsin has a long, prevalent history of papermaking dating back to 1848. In fact, Wisconsin is the number one producer of paper in the United States.

When developing fiber-based solutions, the Ahlstrom-Munksjö Wisconsin plants manufacture products from wood sourced locally in their Midwestern (Wisconsin and Upper Michigan) wood basket. This enables the plants to lower their logistics impact while also supporting the local economies. In addition, the plants are triple Chain-of-Custody Certified through FSC®, SFI® and PEFC™ certifications.

"We are proud of the positive end-of-life story our products have," Addie Teeters, Head of Marketing and Communications, states. "By producing these innovative green products, we are pushing the marketplace to adopt more sustainable options instead of their otherwise plastic counterparts."

"A great example of our renewable solutions includes our Cristal™ transparent packaging papers. Our heat-sealed Cristal™ product received the How2Recycle® Certification from Western Michigan University, and is a great example of us pushing the boundaries of what paper can do," explained Zack Leimkuehler, Vice President of Ahlstrom-Munksjö's Technical Solutions business. "Incorporating these sustainability attributes takes the guesswork out for consumers. The end goal is for consumers to easily know exactly what can be recycled and what cannot." Ahlstrom-Munksjö's products retain their integrity through heat and water, which differentiates them from most in this space. These are just a few of the many examples why Ahlstrom-Munksjö continues to be a leader and pioneer in the paper industry.

"We are constantly asking ourselves how we can innovate the next plastic replacement product, create a more positive end-of-life story for a package, or challenge our sustainability practices in manufacturing and forestry," Teeters further explained. "There is so much specialty paper products can do, and leveraging our historical methods has been extremely rewarding."

Ahlstrom-Munksjö is a global leader in fiber-based materials, supplying innovative and sustainable solutions to its customers. Their mission is to expand the role of fiber-based solutions for sustainable everyday life. Their offering includes filter materials, release liners, food and beverage processing materials, décor papers, abrasive and tape backings, electrotechnical paper, glass fiber materials, medical fiber materials, diagnostics and energy storage solutions as well as a range of specialty papers for industrial and consumer end-uses. You can learn more at www.ahlstrom-munksjo.com.

 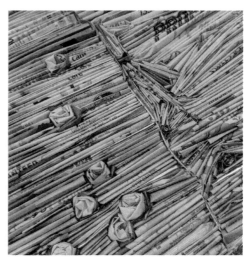

Propcorn, 2020, by Eco Artivist, Francesca Busca. 100% crisp and
popcorn packets, 50 x 50 x 6 cm, from Adobe's 'trashure', first
piece (of five) for their Art for Trash project, where she
makes artworks for the office with their own waste.

TREET: RECOMMERCE FOR ECOMMERCE BRANDS, MAKING SECONDHAND FIRSTHAND

Did you know that the fashion industry creates around 8-10% of global greenhouse gas carbon emissions each year? According to an article in BBC Future, that industry uses more energy than international shipping and flights combined.

Since this is such a large contributor to global warming and the amount of greenhouse gas emissions released each year, companies are starting to create solutions within the fashion industry. Treet, a recommerce platform for helping e-commerce brands launch official resale experience, aims to help reduce greenhouse gasses by offering a solution to keep clothing in circulation longer. Statistically, only 5-7% of resalable fashion is actually being resold as disclosed in a report by BoF Insights.

Jake Disraeli, the Co-Founder and CEO of Treet stated, "We want to make secondhand feel more like firsthand and make that your first path," helping companies set up resale for their businesses and in addition to allowing consumers to create alerts to be notified of secondhand shopping finds

online. He said, "It's ok to not be the most environmentally conscious consumer, but if you're curious and learning, developing slightly new habits, and asking the right questions, that's the best attribute you can have." Disraeli further explains that to positively impact the world in addition to consumer buying power, you need to look at how you can create an amazing business that can develop and grow and also create a lot of good for the world.

Treet's slogan, "Be more circular and reach new customers," and "Reduce your brand's environmental impact in a meaningful way," intends to help e-commerce brands be more sustainable and increase customer loyalty through resale to help consumer brands grow and thrive.

PRODUCT LIFESPAN

Presented with the problem of how apparel brands can be more sustainable, reduce carbon emissions, and keep items out of landfills and in circulation a little bit longer, Treet stepped in with a solution. The founders poured their energy into creating a platform that has potential to create a bigger impact than just a financial impact, to positively impact the world. Disraeli stated that, "How you extend the life of a product in resale and keep items in circulation longer, is one of the best things you can do to reduce its carbon emissions, to give it a longer life." Although a true circular supply chain begins with sourcing sustainable raw materials, setting up manufacturing processes with ethical and eco-friendly principles, and planning for a product's end of life to recycle or repurpose, recommerce is a means to continue that circle of product life. In addition, the push from consumers who want to be more sustainable and learn how to be more environmentally conscious is gaining momentum.

Wolven Pre-Loved

The future of fashion is circular — extend the lifespan of your Wolven pieces by buying or selling pre-loved.

| Shop | Sell |

Wolven Pre-Loved   Buying   Selling   Support   About Treet   Treet Protection

Circular Fashion

HOW RECOMMERCE WORKS

In order to make recommerce easily accessible for all ecommerce apparel brands, Treet creates an online platform that syncs with your existing website, handling everything from tech issues to customer support needed for seller returns and buyer purchases of secondhand items. Easy to print labels, product verification and payments are all handled by the Treet team. Ecommerce brands can set up resale for payments or even store credits or discounts. This offering allows brands to sell items at a discounted rate making their goods more accessible. Current statistics share that 40% of shoppers that purchase from Treet resale partners are new customers to the brand. Recommerce and making secondhand firsthand provides a positive solution for frequent shoppers, ecommerce growth, and progression of environmental efforts.

Sources:
"Can fashion ever be sustainable?" -Smart Guide to Climate Change, BBC Future, https://www.bbc.com/future/article/20200310-sustainable-fashion-how-to-buy-clothes-good-for-the-climate
"The Future of Fashion Resale Report-BoF Insights." The Business of Fashion, https://www.businessoffashion.com/reports/retail/the-future-of-fashion-resale-report-bof-insights
Treet, www.treet.co
Boyish Jeans, www.boyish.com
Wolven, wolventhreads.com

Photography by Steve Brandt.

COUNTING CORAL: OCEAN CONSERVATIONISTS CREATING UNDERWATER SCULPTURES

by Brooke Hodgson

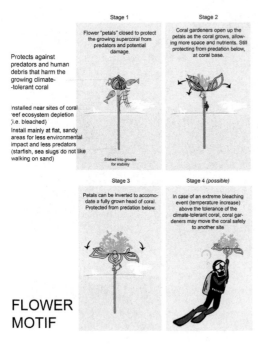

Stage 1
Flower "petals" closed to protect the growing supercoral from predators and potential damage.

Stage 2
Coral gardeners open up the petals as the coral grows, allowing more space and nutrients. Still protecting from predation below, at coral base.

Protects against predators and human debris that harm the growing climate-tolerant coral

Installed near sites of coral reef ecosystem depletion (i.e. bleached)

Install mainly at flat, sandy areas for less environmental impact and less predators (starfish, sea slugs do not like walking on sand)

Staked into ground for stability

Stage 3
Petals can be inverted to accomodate a fully grown head of coral. Protected from predation below.

Stage 4 (possible)
In case of an extreme bleaching event (temperature increase) above the tolerance of the climate-tolerant coral, coral gardeners may move the coral safely to another site

FLOWER MOTIF

The ocean bears the brunt of consumerism, with chemical spills, plastic pollution, overfishing, surface run-off, deoxygenation from fertilizers, and deep sea mining, being just a few of the immediate consequences. This careless behavior has caused a rapid increase in ocean acidification, ocean warming, changes to biological processes, and the death of countless sea ocean plant life and mammals. Coral reefs - our most diverse and fragile ecosystems on the planet, have suffered severely, and we have limited time to save them.

At the forefront of marine deterioration is the fragile reef ecosystem. Known as the rainforest of the sea, coral reefs are the most diverse of all marine ecosystems. Corals provide three-dimensional

structure and substrate to house and feed fish and other marine animals that humans eat. In one way or another, more than 500 million people depend on coral reefs for food, income, coastal protection, and more.

Healthy coral ranges in color including olive green, yellow, blue, pink and dark or light brown coloring. The pigmentation has protective qualities against sunlight and other forms of damaging stress factors. When a coral is dying, it loses its color and becomes white.

Coral reef plants and animals are important sources of new medicines being developed to treat cancer, arthritis, human bacterial infections, Alzheimer's disease, heart disease, viruses, and other diseases. As stationary animals, corals have evolved

to have chemical defenses against predators. These chemical substances are used for research in their medicinal potential and the possibility of nutritional, cosmetic, and larger scaled medicinal treatments.

In contradiction to their outstanding abilities, coral reefs are dying at an alarming rate all over the world. With stressors such as pollution, overfishing, and human-caused ocean warming, 50 percent of the world's coral reefs have died in the last 30 years and up to 90 percent may die within the next century. Very few pristine coral reefs still exist, and we are racing against time to change the statistics. With extreme urgency to restore the reefs, Counting Coral's mission is to plant coral and save

what is left of these beautiful ecosystems. With limited time to make drastic changes, Counting Coral is taking actionable steps to diminish the devastating effects of coral loss by changing the way coral gardeners garden coral.

Counting Coral is leading the development of Sculptural Coral Banks, a new and advanced method to aid coral growth. Sculptural coral banks are designed with coral propagation in mind. These beautiful structures are multi-functional, tackling previous issues in restoration and tourism. Our sculptures are planted out with climate-resilient coral, developing into a coral bank over time.

Our coral banks will naturally propagate reef systems, whilst maintaining a healthy coral supply for harvesting when needed. This process starts with first identifying and harvesting climate resilient coral, then placing these climate resilient corals on our sculptures and allowing them to grow to spawning maturity.

Allowing the coral to grow and spawn in a safe environment will greatly increase the chances of natural propagation. This new technique of coral propagation alleviates the stressors and flaws in all other restoration methods. In addition, this technique can be largely scaled, giving the reefs a chance to survive the race against time.

Counting Coral's sculptures are made from marine-grade stainless steel, which is a durable and non-corrosive material. Differing from most coral gardening practices, Counting Coral's structures are not only practical, but are beautifully designed, and add a visually appealing aesthetic to the underwater world.

Worldwide government initiatives have been set; by the year 2030, 30% of oceans will have been protected. This is a great overall plan, but with current findings, marine protected areas may be "protected" on paper, but evidence shows very little protection and even less management of the area. This is where we differ, as Counting Coral and surrounding communities become stakeholders of these parks - thus being able to manage and protect.

The beautifully designed sculptural installations create meaningful ways to engage individuals with the mission to conserve coral and marine life. Counting Coral strives to positively influence and educate individuals on how to better care for the planet.

Counting Coral's projects are entirely financed by the general public, individual philanthropy, sponsors, and small and large businesses. Our nonprofit model is that all donations go directly into the reef restoration projects, as every penny makes the world of difference. With no direct product to market, driving awareness and raising funds is difficult for a nonprofit.

We would not be able to restore the dying reefs, get materials for the sculptural coral nursery, install and protect what is left of the coral ecosystem, without donations. Environmental protection is an individual responsibility for all human beings. Losing large portions of the natural world will drastically reduce the human quality of life, threatening your children and your children's children.

No species that destroys its own habitat has a chance of survival. There isn't a way to get "out of" taking care of the environment, nor should there be. The more of the planet we contaminate and destroy, the more valuable the remaining areas become; eventually to be exploited and consumed. If we do not learn to live harmoniously with our planet, we will eventually out-consume our ability to sustain ourselves. Be conscious of everything you do and everything you consume. Take the extra second, the extra minute. There is a ticking clock, and we don't want to know what it's like when it runs out.

A before and after series in Schuld, Germany,
before the flood of July 2021.

A before and after series in Schuld, Germany,
after the flood of July 2021.

RECLAIMED WOOD FOR SUSTAINABLE ART

Ike Wynter is the co-founder of Green Up Solutions, a recycled materials family business, and a wood artist. He creates handcrafted woodwork made out of 100% recycled material, creating art using products that would have otherwise entered the waste stream. Ike shares that sustainability is in his blood, but he also understands that it can take time to shift perspective and try to live more sustainably. He encourages others to look at their surroundings and think about how to transform what you already have. One can't become plastic-free overnight, but it's important to start with the things that are most common and easiest to cut out of your life, like cutting out plastic bags and plastic bottles to start.

Applying that mentality to his work, Ike wanted to rethink art in a new way, to change the way people think about the why of a piece. Just like consumerism and comparable to vintage fashion, taking products that already exist and putting it back into the market is impactful. Ike said, "Each time you buy something new, a truck goes out to ship it to you, and many materials like glue are used to create it."

In his eco and sustainable wood wall art, reclaimed wood is used without any additional color, paint, or stain. Instead of using glue for his pieces, nails are used to secure the designs. About 80% of the wood he uses is from old pallets, where other wood scraps come from fences, cabinets, dressers, and even old work benches. Ike also utilizes the wood for the texture and color it already has, selecting wood scraps

He explains that you can make anyone's day better by sharing your story or words of encouragement on whatever avenue or platform you use. Ike commits to replying to every message he receives, wanting to provide value and carry on a conversation. With this opportunity to engage with others, he wants to educate people on the art and environmental sustainability practices of his businesses. Ike said, "Art is my vessel to speak to people," and he's excited for the day when an art show will consist of all reclaimed work.

to design pieces from his sketches or commissioned pieces for individuals and businesses, selling them on his Etsy shop WynterWoodsCo.

THE IMPACT OF ART

Ike encourages everyone to live life every day by keeping your eyes open for opportunities, and being conscious that you can have more of an impact in this world than you realize. Through his Instagram community and anyone that takes interest in his work, Ike aims to provide value through words and inspiration.

Kitch-iti-kipi in Manistique, Michigan, a large
natural spring, meaning "big cold spring" in the
Ojibwe language. Photography by Joe Krubsack.

Giant the
Chickadee, by
Louise Ellwood
Parker, acrylic
paint and ink
on driftwood.

PELVIC HEALTH: THE SECRET TO WOMEN'S WELLBEING

by Megan Rorabeck, DPT, WCS, & Molly Sommerhalder;
photography by Shaena Ragna Photography & Steve Brandt

Our pelvic floor is the connector to our overall wellbeing. When we focus on this part of our body, we can hone in on our overall wellness and focus on the preventive care that we need for longevity. To have an overall healthy life, we need movement, rest, fresh air, mental clarity, and healthy foods. Not only will we lead a better life by focusing on these core practices, but our pelvic floor will also benefit! The pelvic floor is composed of three layers of muscles and provides space for the bladder, uterus and ovaries, and the bowels. Thus, it plays a key role in wellness. For example, we have energy to move because our colon aids in digestion, fresh air helps provide us with mental clarity and offers a space for movement and relaxation, and healthy foods help to balance our hormones. When we find mental and physical balance, our body, and thus our muscles, are flexible yet strong- including those of the pelvic floor.

WHAT IS THE PELVIC FLOOR?

Many women, believe it or not, are quite unfamiliar with this part of their body. The pelvic floor sits between the hips, within the pelvis. It is a group of muscles that span from the pubic bone in the front to the tailbone in the back, and out to the sides of the pelvis at the sit-bones. These muscles encompass the clitoris, urethral opening, vaginal opening, and rectal opening. These muscles are responsible for maintaining continence so that we do not leak urine, stool, or gas; providing stability and support to the pelvis, hips, and low back; aiding in orgasms and sexual stimulation; and promoting blood flow to the pelvis for healthy tissues. For the pelvic floor to function optimally, we need to have balance- not only physically but mentally. The head and pelvis are very closely related as they both hold openings to the body. The head has openings at the ears, nose, and mouth while the pelvis has openings at the urethra, vagina, and rectum. Due to this, these two areas often follow suit: if we have neck tension, clench or grind our teeth, feel stressed, anxious or nervous, then it is likely that our pelvic floor is also in a state of tension. This is why our mental health and mental clarity are so important when addressing pelvic health. We must strike a balance!

PREVENTATIVE CARE FOR OUR PELVIC FLOOR

There are many simple things we can do to keep our pelvic floor healthy. To do this, we must address all components of the pelvic floor: the bladder, bowel, sexual health, and the muscles. The bladder is a muscular organ that should be under voluntary control. In the physical therapy world, we encourage people to demonstrate 'mind over bladder.' Again, the mind-body connection to the pelvic floor is astounding. If you are one that struggles with bladder leakage, urgency, or frequency, you may find that if you are panicked or fearful when you experience a bladder urge, your symptoms become heightened. If you can try and stay calm and in control, you may find that these symptoms quiet down. In addition to regaining control over your bladder, there are ways to set your bladder up for success. For example, drinking water is key as this is a bladder-friendly fluid as compared to fluids that are acidic (orange juice or tomato juice), carbonated, caffeinated, or contain alcohol, which are known to irritate the bladder. Aim to space your water evenly throughout the day for a continuous influx of a bladder-friendly fluid. Additionally, try to avoid going to the bathroom 'just in case' and know that normal voiding frequency during the day is every two to four hours. If you go to the bathroom 'just in case', it can contribute to poor bladder habits.

To optimize bowel health, it is important to drink enough water, eat a well-balanced diet, and exercise. Remember, when you move, your bowels move. Normal bowel movement frequency can be anywhere from three times a day to three times a week. The bowels are very trainable and if you struggle with having bowel movements, try to establish a routine where you allow yourself up to ten minutes to sit on the toilet and relax. Over time, your body will begin to understand that this is the time to have a bowel movement. Warm liquids and chewing your food fully can also help promote bowel movements. If you find that you struggle with bowel leakage, constipation, incomplete bowel emptying, excessive straining to empty, or inability to control gas, you would benefit from an appointment with a pelvic floor physical therapist, as these issues are never normal.

To optimize sexual health, we have to feel a sense of desire along with feeling comfortable and safe, and we need to have healthy pelvic floor tissue. There are many modes a woman can experience an orgasm: vaginal penetration, clitoral stimulation, nipple stimulation, or erratic thoughts. There is no right or wrong or standard as to how an orgasm is achieved. Additionally, you do not need a partner to experience an orgasm or optimize sexual health, as these needs can be met through masturbation. Regardless of the route to achieve an orgasm and if it is done solo or with a partner, it is imperative that you feel comfortable and safe- this goes back to the mind-body connection. If you do not feel safe or comfortable, your body will be unable to fully relax, which may contribute to discomfort or pain during the process.

Healthy tissues will enhance our sexual health and our sexual health will enhance our tissues. With vaginal penetration, the pelvic floor muscles need to be able to relax and lengthen. When experiencing an orgasm, our pelvic floor muscles contract faster and faster until the euphoric orgasm sensation is achieved. During these moments, the pelvic floor tissues experience a surge in blood flow which carries oxygen and nutrients to help keep these tissues healthy. As you can see, the pelvic floor muscles need to have adequate range of motion and flexibility to optimize the sexual experience. Additionally, the sexual experience can be more pleasurable when our tissues are healthy and adequately lubricated, so don't be afraid to use lubricant liberally.

Contrary to what many women have been told, there is much more to keeping your pelvic floor muscles healthy than doing Kegels. The pelvic floor muscles need to be able to squeeze to engage to prevent leakage and provide support to the pelvic organs. Just as importantly as squeezing, they need to be able to relax and lengthen to allow complete bladder and bowel emptying and to accommodate vaginal penetration for use of tampons or menstrual cups, pelvic exams, and penetration for penetrative intercourse. Kegels are only appropriate to do if the pelvic floor muscles can also fully rest and lengthen. If the muscles are in a tense or painful state, Kegels are not appropriate but rather, a lengthening program is warranted. If you are unsure if Kegels are appropriate for you or not, consider seeing a pelvic floor physical therapist who can perform an assessment and provide a specific program based on your needs.

YOGA AND MINDFULNESS FOR OUR PELVIC FLOOR

Yoga and mindfulness are also great tools to keep the pelvic floor healthy and strong. Yoga allows us to open congested areas and create movement to find flexibility and strength in the pelvic floor. There are a variety of poses and practices specific to the pelvic floor. By practicing these on a regular basis, you can lengthen and strengthen your lower body muscles for better mobility. Yoga can also allow us to connect to ourselves on a deeper level so we can truly understand what is happening mentally, physically, and emotionally in this area. Our energy of life flows fully when we open up this part of our body.

Yoga, breath work, and mindfulness techniques, like meditation, movement, mantra and more, can help decrease stress to aid with issues like bladder urgency, bladder frequency, and bladder leakage. Additionally, there are a variety of breath work options available to engage the whole body. The many variations of practices can stimulate digestion, relax our mind and nervous system, and create space for deeper connection to our internal wellbeing.

Some will argue that the pelvic floor is the center of our body as it connects the upper body to the lower body. We can consider the pelvic floor a sacred space and the root of our wellbeing. This space holds the knowledge, wisdom, and curiosity for us to be passionate, creative, and find true embodiment to love ourselves deeply. Due to its vital role in all aspects of our life, it is important we take time to love, nurture, and care for our pelvic floor! If you are curious in learning more, check out Swan in the Lotus Wellness embodiment coaching and yoga and Between the Hips: A Practical Guide for Women, available on Amazon.

Connections, 2021,
by Eco Artivist,
Francesca Busca.

100% rubbish, 50 x 50 cm:
10 years' worth of unwanted
cables, unclaimed or refused
by the various network
providers. Yet in her
eyes, true trashure.

HOLISTIC CARE VIA TELEMEDICINE: THE BEST OF ALL WORLDS

by Dr. Tiffany Mullen

Over the last two years, many of us have had the experience of seeing a doctor by video. Certain health problems we thought never could have been solved by a telemedicine visit were simply and easily managed with the touch of a button. For people who seek integrative and functional medicine care, many of us have been wondering: should I receive my care virtually, even when I don't "have to"?

First, let's define integrative and functional medicine. These areas of specialization in medicine focus on solving health problems (instead of covering symptoms with prescriptions), by getting at the root of the problem. Physicians who practice integrative and functional medicine have additional training beyond medical school and residency in order to be able to provide patients with choices in their care. In-depth lab testing is used to uncover issues that are often missed by traditional health care. Doctors who practice integrative and functional medicine focus on "natural first" whenever possible, but do sometimes prescribe medications when appropriate. Lifestyle is a big focus of integrative and functional medicine, including nutrition, movement, sleep, and managing stress. Now, let's define telemedicine. Generally speaking, a telemedicine visit is defined by seeing a clinician (usually a doctor, but also nurse practitioners, physician assistants, psychologists, and health practitioners are included) via a computer, smart phone, or similar electronic device. In some states, a telemedicine visit can also be defined by having a consultation by phone without video images. Some chat visits via texting may also apply.

Telemedicine has been around for decades, but use has dramatically increased over the last couple of years, mostly because of COVID-19. It is estimated that as of this writing, there has been a 38x increase in telemedicine visits from April, 2020. It is estimated that approximately 70% of all medical conditions can be managed by telemedicine visits. While it is pretty obvious that certain health problems do not lend themselves well to a telemedicine visit (traumatic injuries and surgeries, for example), many conditions are quite safely managed via video. So, conditions are able to be managed via telemedicine, but is it safe? Let me explain.

Doctors of all types are trained to listen to the patient and ask probing questions. The adage in medicine is that 90% of the diagnosis comes from the patient's story. If your story raises concern about something that can't be effectively evaluated via video, the clinician can send you for additional testing or for an in-person evaluation. In that way, your clinician always has an ear tuned for "red flags" and the need for further evaluation. That said, many health issues lend themselves perfectly to a telemedicine approach. Diagnosis and management of hormone imbalance, thyroid conditions, gut health problems, mild depression and anxiety, fertility issues, food sensitivities, and even some more chronic issues like Lyme Disease can be managed via telemedicine.

Conversely, health problems that are quite severe and that require routine monitoring--such as significant heart failure or severe asthma--would not be well-managed in a telemedicine-only approach. There are many advantages to seeing a physician via telemedicine. Functional medicine, by definition, seeks to find the root cause of health conditions, and solve them, instead of covering symptoms with prescriptions. To do this, we take adequate time to evaluate patients, with most functional medicine consultations being much longer than traditional medical visits. The majority of this assessment is a conversation between the patient and the practitioner, so that naturally works well for video visits. Additionally, for many people, finding a functional medicine clinician close to their home can be challenging. Having the ability to access a functional medicine provider from home via telemedicine eliminates that issue. Lastly, many functional medicine practitioners have special skills or training in certain areas, such as hormones, fertility, or gut health. However, that specialized clinician may not be in your neighborhood or even in your state. Being able to access the best practitioner for you leads to the best opportunity for you to get your health back.

About Vytal Health: Founded in 2018, Vytal Health was created to help patients seeking integrative and functional medicine find and work with the best physician to help them overcome their health problems. Our model provides extensive support, from your own care concierge to help you navigate, to your physician, nutritionist, and health coach: the entire team wraps around each patient in a personalized way. Overcoming health challenges and making lifestyle changes isn't easy, but thankfully seeing your health care team via video from the comfort of home is. No more being rushed and dismissed by a doctor who doesn't bother to get to know you. No more waiting rooms. No more prescriptions for every symptom. We believe every patient deserves to be heard. Vytal Heatlh: Better health. Better Care.

Photography by Steve Brandt.

RETURNING TO A LIFE OF HOPE AFTER MAJOR LIFE CHANGE

by Amanda Hofacker; artwork by Francesca Busca

There are two known truths in this life: we are born on an inhale, and we depart on an exhale. The space between those two breaths is the great mystery we call our lives. Every piece is a journey where we learn to navigate our tragedies and grievances throughout the many chapters. It may seem like "that phone call" will never come, that accident or diagnosis will never happen, but we simply cannot know how it will all unfold, and from this mystery we can learn to approach life with reverence and bow to the uncertainty of it all.

Regeneration, 2022, by Eco Artivist, Francesca Busca. Commission for the main lobby of a global financial services firm in NYC, made from 100% waste: about 2,000 metal screw caps and just as many ring pulls, 120 x 90 cm, and 6 months of slow but steady collection.

The first time I sat with the part of life I didn't believe would actually ever come for me was when I watched my dad die. When I watched his fragile, delicate body slowly start to depart, and when he finally took his last breath, I remember being frozen in a trance, a dream-like state of sorts, at the uncertainty and fragility and reminder of my own immortality and how temporary this all is. After the haze lifted, I came to see that grief is everywhere, everyone is grieving, and no one escapes grief if they've lived and loved deeply. And from that shared experience, I began to see beauty and identified immense hope from this tragedy that we all share together. That's what I remind myself on darker days, hope is the reminder that we aren't alone in any of this.

Almost one year ago today, I fell ill with some peculiar symptoms and finally sought out a doctor who ran blood work. While waiting for my results, I assumed, like always, that everything would come back normal and eventually my symptoms would lift and life would resume as it always had. My doctor said she would follow up with me in a few weeks, so when she called two days later at 8:01 am, I was reluctant to answer the call. When she told me that I was at near death levels for ketoacidosis and hyperglycemia, and that I had Type 1 diabetes, an autoimmune disorder that causes the destruction of all insulin producing cells in the body, I felt myself entering that same detached, dream-like state that I had entered when I watched my dad take his last breath. This can't be real. How can my body be dying? I was an otherwise healthy 34-year-old woman who practiced yoga, hiked, and ate mostly organic food. She told me that my life would never be the same, and that I would have to take multiple shots of insulin everyday for the rest of my life, and that if I didn't take this disease seriously and put in the work, that I would suffer from a long list of terrifying complications like limb loss, blindness, cancer, heart disease, stroke, kidney failure, or premature death. No one tells you about the grief you experience when your own body fails you. No one talks about the shame you experience when your own body fails you. And very few understand the full-time, 24/7-hour day job, without any pay, that you put in to manage chronic illness. The cost. The endless medical appointments. The fear.

I spent the better part of the next 3 months in the deepest state of depression. At one point I convinced myself that I did indeed want to die because I wasn't going to take pharmaceutical insulin for the rest of my life to survive. It seemed unnatural- if my body wanted to die- fine, let it die. I grieved the relationship, passion, and love I used to have for food and was consumed by numbers and the endless math equation that diabetes is. Every time someone said, "Wow, I can't believe you're diabetic, did you eat a lot of sugar as a child?" I cringed and the well of shame grew deeper. Then came the medical devices, the insulin pump and the glucose monitor, and while they made living with the disease so much easier, they were also visible reminders that it was real.

I don't remember exactly when I started to come back home to myself, or back to life, but I remember one day letting go of some of the battle and coming to a place of radical acceptance. This body had been begging me all of my life to love it; I never listened. And now more than ever, my body was pleading to be loved, pleading to be cared for. And for the first time in my life, I said, "Okay, I'm going to really love you." And just like the grief I had experienced when I lost my dad, when I looked out into the world, I saw that there were so many other warriors out there. That every person and every body lives with something. And these beautiful, strong warriors, who had been through so much with their own bodies, with illness, grief, injury, and near-death experiences, came to my rescue and reminded me once again, you are not alone. We are not alone. So that's my big revelation, my big reveal on how I turned back to seeing the world and my body as a hopeful place- by looking out and recognizing the story that everyone carries.

On an everyday level I think it's also important to utilize virtual or in-person platforms of support. I follow several Instagram accounts by people who live with Type 1 who are thriving and living full, healthy, and adventurous lives. They hold space for mutual understanding and hardship, but also remind their followers that having a chronic disease shouldn't hold you back from doing the things that you love. A big portion of my healing process over the past year has also involved incorporating activities and rituals that activate the parasympathetic nervous system (rest and digest, tend and befriend) and nourish the adrenals. Life disrupting events, like experiencing the death of a loved one, job loss, divorce, or dealing with long-term illness, are extremely taxing on the body and mind, often leading to things like adrenal fatigue and HPA- Axis dysfunction from the trauma of the experience. The systems and tissues of our bodies hold traumatic experiences within them so anything that can help us somatically release these experiences, including working with a somatic therapist, can be incredibly helpful. Other tools and exercises that I've found helpful and try to incorporate on a regular basis are breath work, meditation, gentle yoga (especially Yin), walks in nature, getting plenty of sunshine, establishing healthier sleeping patterns, and incorporating nourishing foods and vitamins that help rebuild the body like vitamins C & D3, and probiotics. It is often necessary after experiencing a traumatic experience to tune into states of deeper rest that involve less activity or obligations, always remembering that your body will intuitively guide you with what it needs.

Gaztelugatxe Island in Basque Country in northern Spain.
Photography by Stephanie Krubsack.

WHITE TEA HEALTH BENEFITS

by Jennifer Nowicki; photography by Alexis Arnold

In the East tea has been known to be the key to good health, happiness, and wisdom for thousands of years. Most people in the West know that green tea can be very healthy for you, but many are just starting to understand that all tea is healthy unless you or the company that blends the tea adds something unhealthy to it. As oolong tea has been gaining more followers in the United States since COVID hit, white and pu-erh teas have been getting more and more popular as well. This should continue because scientists are researching these teas more and finding many great health benefits to them too. In this article I will focus on the health benefits of white tea.

One health benefit of white tea is that it helps promote tooth health. White tea is rich in catechins, tannins, and fluoride, which in turn are properties that are good for the health of your teeth. It helps fight cavities, strengthen tooth enamel, and prevents acid damage caused by bacteria and sugars. The catechins help prevent plaque growth.

Another health benefit of white tea is weight loss. White tea is just as effective in fat burning as green tea and can help you lose weight. Both teas have similar caffeine levels and catechins like EGCGs that are linked to fat burning, where caffeine and EGCG compounds have a synergic effect on weight loss. The nice thing about drinking white tea is if you do not add anything to it, it is calorie free and because it is the least processed it has more antioxidants than most other tea types.

White tea is high in antioxidants and considered one of the best teas to protect the body from free radicals. White tea contains quite a few antioxidants like polyphenols, flavonoids, and tannins that help with chronic health conditions, like heart disease, diabetes, and some cancers. With heart disease being a serious issue in the United States, the leading cause of death, white tea can help reduce the risk of heart disease in several ways. Heart disease is strongly linked to chronic inflammation. White tea has the ability, because of its polyphenols, to relax blood vessels and boost immunity. While other studies state that polyphenols can prevent "bad" LDL cholesterol from being oxidized (another heart disease risk factor). Scientists found that heart disease becomes a 21% lower risk when people drink three or more cups of white tea a day.

Insulin is an important hormone to help nutrients move from the bloodstream into the cells to be stored and used later. If someone consumes large amounts of sugar among other things, it can cause the body to not respond to insulin. This is called insulin resistance and is linked to chronic health conditions like type 2 diabetes, heart disease, and metabolic syndrome. The polyphenols found in white tea lower the risk of insulin resistance. Also, the EGCG and polyphenols prevent high blood sugar levels.

My grandfather died of Alzheimer's, so I always notice when anything can be helpful to lower the risk of getting this disease. White tea's polyphenol EGCGs may lower the risk of Alzheimer's and Parkinson's disease. The EGCGs can suppress the free radicals, reduce inflammation, and reduce other risk factors of both diseases. Eight studies with over 5,600 people found that people who drank white tea had 15% lower risk of Parkinson's disease than those who did not drink white tea. A group of 26 studies with over 52,500 people found that drinking white tea daily lowered the risk of Alzheimer's disease by 35%.

These are just some of the many health benefits of this truly lovely and tasty delicate tea. Research into the health benefits is white tea is still new, so in time scientists may find even more health benefits to drinking white tea.

Sources:
"Meta-Analysis of the Association between Tea Intake and the Risk of Cognitive Disorders." PubMed, https://pubmed.ncbi.nlm.nih.gov/27824892/

Spice Market in Marrakesh, Morocco.
Photography by Stephanie Krubsack.

GLUTEN-FREE VEGAN FRUIT CREPES

by Stephanie Krubsack

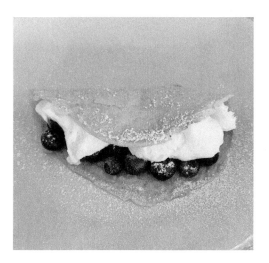

Ingredients:
- 1 tbsp oil (15 g)
- ¼ tsp salt (1.42 g)
- 1 ½ c almond milk (360 g)
- 1 c gluten-free flour (122 g)
- coconut oil for cooking

Toppings:
- powdered sugar
- dairy-free whipped topping
- strawberries, raspberries, blueberries, bananas

Directions:
In a large bowl, beat all ingredients together. Heat a large stovetop pan to medium heat and coat generously with coconut oil. Spoon roughly two large tablespoons of batter onto the pan and spread around until evenly coated. Cook each side for roughly two minutes. Place fruit and cream on one half of the crepe, fill with your favorite fruit, and top with the whipped topping. Fold the other half of the crepe over the fruit and cream. Use a small strainer to sift powdered sugar on top. The recipe makes 8-10 crepes depending on size.

PALEO BANANA CHOCOLATE CHIP MUFFINS

by Cindi Lockhart, RDN, LD, functional nutritionist

Dry Ingredients:
- 1 c almond flour (112 g)
- ½ c arrowroot flour (64 g)
- ¼ c tapioca flour (32 g)
- ¼ c coconut flour (28 g)
- ¾ c sugar substitute (168 g)
  Use any 1:1 ratio sugar substitute, we used Lakanto monk fruit sweetener
- 1 tsp baking powder (4.2 g)
  For 1 tsp (4.2 g) of cornstarch-free baking powder, use ½ tsp (2.84 g) cream of tartar, ¼ tsp (1.42 g) arrowroot, and ¼ tsp (1.42 g) baking soda
- 1 tsp baking soda (4.2 g)
- ½ tsp cinnamon (2.84 g)
- ½ tsp salt (2.84 g)

Wet Ingredients:
- 2 Flax eggs
  Mix 2 tbsp (28.3 g) ground flaxseed meal with 5 tbsp (70.87 g) of water and let set for 10-15 minutes until consistency of eggs
- ⅓ c melted refined coconut oil or grapeseed oil (75 g)
- 2 tsp vanilla extract (11.8 g)
- 1 tbsp apple cider vinegar (15 g)
- 1 c mashed ripe banana (270 g)
- ¾ c sugar-free chocolate chips (120 g) We used Lily's dark chocolate sugar free

PALEO BANANA CHOCOLATE CHIP MUFFINS

by Cindi Lockhart, RDN, LD, functional nutritionist

Directions:

1. Preheat oven to 350° F (176 °C).
2. Make the flax eggs.
3. Grease a 12-cup muffin tray.
4. In a medium bowl mix the oil (melted if using coconut oil), vanilla extract, apple cider vinegar and banana until well blended.
5. In a large bowl, whisk the flours, sugar substitute, baking powder, baking soda, cinnamon, and salt until well blended.
6. Once the flax eggs are ready, add them to the flour mixture along with the banana mixture; fold in the chocolate chips.
7. Fill each muffin cup with about a ¼ cup batter. There will be enough batter for 12 muffins.
8. Bake for 25-30 minutes or until a toothpick inserted into the center comes out clean.
9. Allow to cool completely in the pan, once cooled, use a knife to gently loosen the sides and lift the muffin out of the pan. Store in an airtight container in the refrigerator. These can be enjoyed cold or warmed up.

Recipe Notes:

For a quick bread loaf. lightly grease a 9" x 5" loaf pan. Evenly spread the batter in the pan and bake for 55-60 minutes or until a knife inserted into the center comes out clean. Allow to cool 90 minutes before slicing. Loaf will be slightly fragile, so it's recommended to slice the loaf in the pan. Store in an airtight container in the refrigerator.

Editor's Tip:

Melt extra chocolate chips to drizzle on top of the muffins for decoration, or edible flower petals.

PESTO PIZZA WITH SUN-DRIED TOMATO CRUST

by Stephanie Krubsack

Pizza Crust:
- ½ c sun-dried tomatoes (27 g)
- ¾ c gluten-free flour (96 g)
- 3 tbsp chia seeds (42.52 g)
- 1 c almond flour (112 g)
- ¼ tsp pepper (1.42 g)
- ⅔ c water (158 g)
- ¼ tsp salt (1.42 g)

Pesto:
- salt & pepper to taste
- 3 tbsp olive oil (45 g)
- 2 c spinach (60.1 g)
- ½ c pecans (65 g)

Topping Suggestions:
- dairy-free shredded cheese
- mini heirloom tomatoes
- mushrooms
- peppers
- onions
- fennel
- olives
- basil

Directions:
Finely chop the sun-dried tomatoes or place in a food processor. Mix with other pizza crust ingredients. You may need more water depending on the type of gluten-free flour you use. Grease a pan and pat the dough into a circular or rectangular shape. Prebake the crust at 375° F (190 °C) for 5-10 minutes then remove from the oven.

Mix all pesto ingredients in a food processor. Spread the pesto on the prebaked crust. Add the desired toppings from the options listed. Bake for another 20 minutes or until the cheese is melted and the toppings are golden brown.

JACKFRUIT NO-CRAB CAKES

by Stephanie Krubsack

Brine:
- 1 sheet nori chopped into small pieces (2 sheets if no dulse)
- generous sprinkle of dulse seaweed flakes
- 2 tbsp liquid aminos (30 g)
- enough water to cover

No-Crab Cakes:
- 1 can of jackfruit
- 1 clove garlic
- ½ white onion
- 3 chopped green onions
- 2 tbsp (28.3 g) ground flaxseed meal
- 5 tbsp water (70.87 g)
- 1 c gluten-free bread crumbs (119 g)
- ½ tsp umami seasoning (2.84 g)
- ¼ tsp mustard powder (1.42 g)
- ¼ tsp onion powder (1.42 g)
- ¼ tsp celery salt (1.42 g)
- ½ tsp sea salt (2.84 g)
- dash cayenne pepper
- 1 tsp paprika (4.2 g)
- dash black pepper
- dash nutmeg

Topping:
- ¼ c vegan cream cheese (44 g)
- ¼ c vegan mayonnaise (57.5 g)
- chopped fresh dill

JACKFRUIT NO-CRAB CAKES

by Stephanie Krubsack

Directions:

1. First mix the brine ingredients together in a glass container with a lid and set aside.
2. Drain the jackfruit and smash each piece of with the heel of your hand then chop into thin crab-like strands. Soak the pieces in the brine for 1-2 hours in the refrigerator.
3. Next, finely chop and sauté the green onions (sauté the white part, keep the green separate to mix in with the cakes), garlic and white onion. Set aside.
4. Mix the ground flaxseed meal and 5 tbsp (70.87 g) water in a separate bowl and set aside to rest for 10 minutes.
5. Strain the liquid from the marinating jackfruit (be sure to keep the nori and dulse pieces), mix with the garlic and onions, flaxseed mixture, remaining spices, and breadcrumbs.
6. Form the dough into small patties and bake at 350° F (176 °C) on a greased pan for about 10 minutes on each side.
7. Mix the topping ingredients together and use to garnish with a sprig of dill or use as a dipping sauce.

Pictured is vegan caviar for garnish. The recipe makes roughly 24 bite-sized cakes.

Color and cut out the bookmarks to save your
place as you read. You can paste the bookmark
paper to a piece of cardboard, laminate them, or
place between two pieces of clear packaging
tape for at-home lamination.

HOME OR OFFICE ECO AUDIT

Carbon Emissions | Waste/Trash | Energy Usage

Directions: Check the areas that are already in practice.
Take notes below for areas that you want to take action on!

Carbon Emissions

☐ Offset flight emissions by donating

☐ Track your mileage for emissions

☐ Invest in sustainable funds and companies

☐ Monitor what you buy new and prioritize secondhand

Waste/Trash

☐ Have recycling bins on site

☐ Have a compost bin on site

☐ Count the bags of trash per week

☐ Set a goal to limit single use plastic

Energy Usage

☐ Use LED bulbs and lighting

☐ Monitor your electricity usage

☐ Use energy efficient appliances

☐ Purchase renewable energy if possible

Notes

_____

_____

_____

_____

GIVE BACK

GREAT LAKES

The dawn of a movement

Environment | Society | Economy

photo by: @drew.links

APPENDIX

Ahlstrom-Munksjö
www.ahlstrom-munksjo.com
IG: @ahlstrommunksjo

Alexis Arnold Photography
www.alexisarnoldphotography.com
IG: @aarnoldphotos

Amanda Hofacker
IG: @introvertedyogi1111

Blue Cast Podcast
carvedinblue.tencel.com/podcast
IG: @carvedinblue

CannedWater4Kids
www.cannedwater4kids.org
IG: @cannedwater4kids

Carbonfund.org
IG: @carbonfund.org_foundation

Counting Coral
www.countingcoral.com
IG: @countingcoral

Cradle to Cradle
c2ccertified.org
IG: @cradletocradle.ngo

Devrim Furkan Kavcar
IG: @defukart

Dr. Tiffany Mullen
Vytal Health
vytalhealth.com
IG: @yourvytalhealth

Fox Valley Drone Geek
www.foxvalleydronegeek.com

Francesca Busca
francescabusca.com
IG: @francesca_busca

Fridays For Future
fridaysforfuture.org
IG: @fridaysforfuture

Give Back Great Lakes
www.givebackgreatlakes.org
IG: @givebackgreatlakes

Ike Wynter
Wynter Woods
etsy.com/shop/WynterWoodsCo
IG: @ike_wynter

Jennifer Nowicki
Cultivate Taste Tea
cultivatetaste.com
IG: @cultivatetastetea

Joe Krubsack
Helivue Productions
helivueproductions.com
IG: @helivue_productions

Lenzing Group
www.lenzing.com/lenzing-group
IG: @ecovero_global

Louise Ellwood Parker
www.ellwoodparker.co.uk
IG: @ellwoodparker

APPENDIX

Matthias Heilig
matthias.heilig@posteo.de

Megan Rorabeck
Between the Hips: A Practical
Guide for Women
www.amazon.com/gp/product/0578
727560
IG: @betweenthehips

Milwaukee Riverkeeper
Milwaukeeriverkeeper.org
IG: @mkeriverkeeper

Molly Sommerhalder
Swan in the Lotus Yoga and Wellness
www.slwellness.info
IG: @swan_in_the_lotus

Nicole Conrad
www.conrad-architekten.com

O My Bag
omybag.nl
omybag.nl/pages/eco-friendly-
leather
IG: @omybagamsterdam

Person & Planet Podcast
anchor.fm/personandplanet

Purevant Living
purevantliving.com
IG: @purevantliving

Shaena Ragna Photography
www.shaenaragnaphotography.com
IG: @shaenaragna

Stephanie Krubsack
skparfait.com
IG: @skparfait

Steve Brandt
www.creativecompassionphotography.com
IG: @creativecompassionphoto

TENCEL™
www.tencel.com
carvedinblue.tencel.com
IG: @tencel_usa @tencel_global

Treet
www.treet.co
IG: @treetshop

Wisconsin Sustainable Business Council
www.wisconsinsustainability.com
IG: @wisconsinsustainability

DICTIONARY

Climate justice:
The best definition by B Lab U.S. & Canada, reads that, "Climate justice recognizes that those who are least responsible for climate change are more likely to suffer its most devastating effects, now and in the future. Climate justice places the needs, voices, and leadership of those who are most impacted by climate change at the forefront."

Earth Overshoot Day:
Known as the annual day where the world population consumes the amount of resources available for that year, this day tracks the demand and usage of natural resources, which exceeds what the planet is able to regenerate in one year. This basically means that if we continue to use resources at such a fast rate, we may eventually run out. You can learn more here: www.overshootday.org

Carbon footprint:
This is the amount of CO_2 emissions created from activities that produce carbon emissions such as driving a car, flying, or home energy usage. Manufacturing a product also emits carbon dioxide into the atmosphere from basic operations.

SDGs:
Short for the Sustainable Development Goals, the SDGs are a group of 17 global goals created by the United Nations in 2015. They are: (1) No Poverty, (2) Zero Hunger, (3) Good Health and Well-being, (4) Quality Education, (5) Gender Equality, (6) Clean Water and Sanitation, (7) Affordable and Clean Energy, (8) Decent Work and Economic Growth, (9) Industry, Innovation and Infrastructure, (10) Reduced Inequality, (11) Sustainable Cities and Communities, (12) Responsible Consumption and Production, (13) Climate Action, (14) Life Below Water, (15) Life On Land, (16) Peace, Justice, and Strong Institutions, (17) Partnerships for the Goals. The current initiative is to achieve all goals by 2030. Here is a link for additional information: sdgs.un.org/goals

Cradle-to-cradle design:
This design principle explains the circular approach to look at the life cycle of a product from cradle-to-cradle, where after its use it can return to the earth. Traditional linear production functions as cradle to grave, where the product becomes trash after its intended use. To learn more from the concept creators, you can read, "Cradle to Cradle: Remaking the Way We Make Things," by German chemist Michael Braungart and US architect William McDonough.

Printed in Great Britain
by Amazon

83225880R00045